W9-CGL-946

CONTENTS

Cover Story

"Even the Son of Man did not come to be served. Instead, he came to serve others. He came to give his life as the price for setting many people free."

(Mark 10:45)

8

12

86

CALENDAR

MEMO	SUN	MON	TUE
		1	2
	7	8	9
	14	15	16
	21	22	23
	28	29	30

JAN

WED	THU	FRI	SAT
3	4	5	6
10	11	12	13
17	18	19	20
24	25	26	27
31			

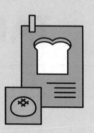

How to Use

1 TODAY'S WORD

This Bible passage is a shortened version of God's Word. You can read the passage in full in your Bible.

2 PREPARE

gives you helpful information about the Bible passage.

Put stickers here as you complete the Bible devotions each day. The stickers can be found at the back of the book.

3 MIX

is a short summary of the Bible passage.

4 MOLD

is a lesson from the Bible passage.

SAT

13

● Mark 5:21–43

Just Believe

PREPARE

* Jairus was a synagogue leader.

sticker

²¹ Jesus went across the Sea of Galilee. [..] ²² Then a man named Jairus [..²³..] begged Jesus, [..] "My little daughter is dying. [..] Heal her." [..] ²⁴ So Jesus went with him. A large group [..] followed. [..] ²⁵ A woman was there who had a sickness that made her bleed. [..] ²⁷ [..] She [..] touched his clothes. ²⁸ She thought, "I just need to touch his clothes. Then I will be healed." ²⁹ [..] Her bleeding stopped. [..] ³⁰ [..] Jesus [..] asked, "Who touched my clothes?" [..] ³³ Then the woman came and [..] `told him. [..] ³⁴ He said to her, [..] "Your faith has healed you. Go in peace." [..] ³⁵ [..] Some people came from the house of Jairus. [..] "Your daughter is dead," they said. [..] ³⁶ Jesus [..] told the synagogue leader, [..] "Just believe." [..] ⁴⁰ [..] He went in where the child was. ⁴¹ He took her by the hand. Then he said to her, "Talitha koum!" This means, "Little girl, I say to you, get up!" ⁴² [..] She stood up. [..] ⁴³ Jesus gave strict orders not to let anyone know what had happened. [..]

MIX

Jairus asks Jesus to come heal his daughter. A large crowd follows Him. Among them is a very sick woman. She touches His clothes thinking this would heal her. Jesus tells her it is her faith that healed her. Meanwhile, Jairus is told his daughter died. Jesus still goes to his house and encourages Jairus to believe. Once there, He tells the girl to get up and she does.

44 MOLD

Believing God is what is required of us as believers. Let us put our wholehearted faith in God in every area of our lives.

Baking is our theme for the year 2024. To make a sweet treat out of God's Word, first PREPARE all the ingredients and MIX them well so that we can have a good understanding of the Bible passage. After that, MOLD the dough into the right shapes as we shape our hearts based on what we learn from His Word and put it into the oven to BAKE it. Then, it's time to TASTE and savor the sweetness of the Word of God! The process ends with a PRAYER to thank God for giving us those delicious words that bring utmost comfort to our soul.

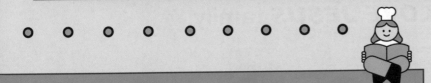

BAKE

Jesus tells the bleeding woman that it is her faith that healed her. Then, he wishes her to ___ ___ _____. (verse 34)

5 BAKE
allows you to explore the text and find answers.

TASTE

What are some things about God that you believe? Write them down below.

I believe God _____.

_____

_____

_____

_____

6 TASTE
allows you to apply the Bible passage into your personal life.

7 PRAYER
allows you to ask for God's help in applying today's Bible passage in your daily life.

PRAYER

Dear God, You are the Healer that heals our physical and spiritual illness. Help me to wholeheartedly believe in You at all times.

45

As Christians, we are a family in Christ. Here are a few members of our *I LOVE JESUS* family!

"When I grow up I want to be a veterinarian because I want to help animals in need."

Lucas Han Liang Ding

- Age: 9
- Singapore
- Faith Community Baptist Church

"When I grow up, I want to become the CEO of a resort or ranch with horses and other animals."

Charlotte Kim

- Age: 6
- Billerica, MA, USA
- Intercultural Mission Church

The Family Page will be uploaded on the I Love Jesus instagram. Please visit instagram.com/ilovejesus_duranno & check it out!

ATTENTION
I LOVE JESUS READERS!

We would like to know who YOU are!
Would you like to appear in our next devotionals?
Please send us a picture of yourself holding your
I LOVE JESUS devotional, preferably on a light background, to:

ilovejesus@duranno.com

provide the following information with your picture:

1. Name

2. Age

3. City/State/Country

4. Church name

5. When I grow up…

★ What do you want to become or achieve when you grow up? Share with us your dreams so that we can pray with you. Please make it no longer than two sentences.

★ Make sure to get permission from your parents first.

★ We will send you a confirmation email once the Family Page containing your picture is ready to be published.

★ Please allow a few months for your picture to be published because we receive several pictures from our readers all around the world!

Written by **Elizabeth Cho**   Illustrated by **Hongbum Chae**

Jenny >

Why Did Jesus Keep His Identity a Secret?

Why did Jesus tell people not to tell others about His miracles and identity?

That's a very good question, Jenny! Did you also know that sometimes Jesus tells people to go and tell everyone what He did and who He is?

Really? Then why does Jesus sometimes want to keep it a secret and sometimes not?! I'm more confused now!

Jesus had very good reasons to keep His work and identity as a secret. As you know, Jesus didn't come to be popular on earth. It was also a matter of timing. Jesus knew the kind of death He had to die. He knew when, where, and how He was to die, so He didn't want His popularity to mess up the timing when He would reveal Himself as the Messiah.

Sorry, but what's the meaning of Messiah?

Messiah means savior. The Jews were awaiting the Messiah for many years.

 So Jesus came to save the Jews only?

No, He came to save all of us from our sins because everyone, whether Jew or not, have fallen short of the glory of God. God used the nation of Israel and their history to bring the Messiah that would save everyone who believes in Him.

Oh, I see! Going back to my question: does that mean that sometimes Jesus told people to tell others about His works and identity because the timing was "right?"

Right Timing

Exactly! Do you know about Palm Sunday?

I heard about it, but I don't remember what it is exactly.

It is when Jesus entered Jerusalem riding on a donkey. At that time, Jesus told His followers to tell others about Him. He did that because He knew the timing was right— He would soon be crucified.

Now I understand everything! So what about now? What should I do?

If you believe in Jesus as the Messiah, you can always ask the Holy Spirit to help you discern when is a good time to talk about Him directly or what is a good time to quietly pray for others to know Him as Messiah.

 So it's all about timing for me as well! I will pray and ask the Holy Spirit to guide me so that I will know when to talk about Jesus and when to quietly pray for others to know Him!

So he said to them, "Those who are healthy don't need a doctor. Sick people do. I have not come to get those who think they are right with God to follow me. I have come to get sinners to follow me."
(Mark 2:17)

The Gospel of Jesus, the Son of God

The Gospel of Mark tells of the ministry of Jesus, who was the Son of God but came to serve sinners. Jesus is the true God who chose to take the sin of the world upon Himself to save people from their sin. The Gospel of Mark proves that Jesus came just as it had been prophesied by Isaiah and in the other Old Testament prophecies.

1. Prepare the way for the Lord

While living in the desert, John the Baptist preached that people should repent and be baptized. People at that time praised John the Baptist. However, he said that the Messiah, who baptizes people with the Holy Spirit, would come, so he encouraged them to repent and prepare the way for Jesus, the Son of God.

In the desert prepare the way for the LORD. Make a straight road through it for our God. (Isaiah 40:3)

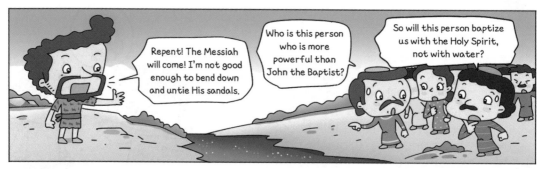

2. The Son of God came as a human

Jesus is the Son of God, but he came as a man to save sinners. That is why John the Baptist baptized Jesus with water before Jesus began His ministry. The Holy Spirit sent Jesus into the desert, and there Satan tempted Jesus.

3. Jesus' miracles and the Good News

Jesus began His ministry by proclaiming the kingdom of God. He performed amazing miracles to let people know what it would be like to live in the kingdom of God as His saved people. As Isaiah prophesied, Jesus freed those who had suffered from fear, sickness, and sin by preaching the gospel of heaven.

The Spirit of the LORD and King is on me. The LORD has anointed me to announce good news to poor people. He has sent me to comfort those whose hearts have been broken. He has sent me to announce freedom for those who have been captured. He wants me to set prisoners free from their dark cells.

(Isaiah 61:1)

4. Jesus came as a servant

Jesus said that anyone who wanted to be first must be the very last and should be the servant of everyone. Jesus came to serve people and sacrificed Himself to save them from sin. Jesus told His disciples to serve others with faith like that of a little child.

5. Jesus chose to die the death of a sinner

Jesus shared bread and wine with His disciples and told them to remember His body and blood, which would be poured out for them. Like a flawless lamb for Passover, Jesus shed His innocent blood on the cross so that we could be saved and escape death.

6. Jesus went up to heaven

As He had foretold His disciples, Jesus died on the cross and rose from the dead. He conquered death, broke the power of demons and all sins, and gained ultimate victory. So if anyone believes in Jesus, they will receive the gift of eternal life and no longer be slaves of sin. Jesus, who sits on the right side of God, would always be with His disciples.

Jesus, who is sitting on the right side of God, lives forever.
He is praying for all of us. As you read and meditate on the Gospel of Mark, remember that Jesus will always be with you, as He was with His disciples.

BIBLE JUMBLE

GOOD

BEGINNING

MESSIAH

NEWS

This is the _____ of the ____ ____ about Jesus the _____.

(Mark 1:1)

The answer key is on page 100.

WEEK

1

We memorize things quicker when we write them out. To help you memorize this week's memory verse, write out the Bible verse below.

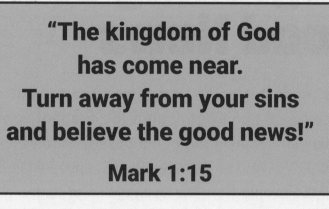

> **"The kingdom of God
> has come near.
> Turn away from your sins
> and believe the good news!"**
>
> **Mark 1:15**

"The kingdom of God
has come near.
Turn away from your sins
and believe the good news!"

Mark 1:15

01

Mark 1:1–15

Beginning of the Good News

PREPARE

* Messiah means anointed or chosen one.

sticker

[1] This is the beginning of the good news about Jesus the Messiah. [...] [2] Long ago Isaiah the prophet wrote, [...] [3] "A messenger is calling out in the desert, 'Prepare the way for the Lord.'" [...] [4] And so John the Baptist appeared in the desert. [...] [5] All the people from the countryside of Judea went out to him. [...] John baptized them in the Jordan River. [...] [7] Here is what John was preaching, [...] "There is someone coming who is more powerful than I am. [...] [8] [...] He will baptize you with the Holy Spirit." [9] At that time Jesus came. [...] John baptized Jesus. [...] [11] A voice spoke to him from heaven, [...] "You are my Son, and I love you." [...] [12] At once the Holy Spirit sent Jesus out into the desert. [13] He was in the desert 40 days. There Satan tempted him. [...] Angels took care of him. [14] [...] Jesus went into Galilee. He preached. [...] [15] "The time has come," he said. [...] "Turn away from your sins and believe the good news!"

MIX

Isaiah had prophesied that a messenger would prepare the way of the Messiah. This person is John the Baptist. He tells people that a greater man than him will baptize them with the Holy Spirit. When Jesus is baptized, God declares that Jesus is His Son. Afterwards, Jesus is tempted by Satan in the desert for 40 days. Once that time is finished, He goes to preach the good news in Galilee.

MOLD

Jesus' call to turn away from our sins and believe the good news still resonates today. Let us confess and turn away from our sins and believe Jesus is our Messiah.

BAKE

John said Jesus would baptize people with the Holy _____. Fill in the correct letters to spell out the answer. (verse 8)

QSMPXYRBILTA

TASTE

As you start this year, write down some goals you want to reach as someone who knows the good news about Jesus.

PRAYER

Dear Jesus, thank you for bringing the kingdom of God to us. Help me to turn away from my sins and fill me with the Holy Spirit so that I may love you.

TUE

02

Mark 1:16–34

Calling and Following

PREPARE

* Simon, Andrew, James and John are fishermen.

sticker

16 [...] Jesus [...] saw Simon and his brother Andrew. [...] 17 [...] "Follow me," Jesus said. [...] 18 At once they [...] followed him. 19 Then Jesus [...] saw James [...] and his brother John. [...] 20 Right away he called out to them. [...] They followed Jesus. 21 Jesus [...] went to Capernaum. [...] He went into the synagogue. There he began to teach. [...] 23 Just then a man [...] controlled by an evil spirit [...] said, 24 [...] "Have you come to destroy us?" [...] 25 "Be quiet!" said Jesus firmly. "Come out of him!" 26 The evil spirit [...] came out of him. [...] 27 All the people were amazed. [...] 28 News about Jesus spread. [...] 29 Jesus [...] went [...] to the home of Simon and Andrew. 30 Simon's mother-in-law was lying in bed with a fever. [...] Jesus [...] 31 [...] helped her up. The fever left her. [...] 32 That evening, [...] the people brought to Jesus all who were sick. [...] 34 Jesus healed many. [...] He also drove out many demons. [...]

MIX

Jesus calls Simon, Andrew, James, and John to follow Him. They go into a synagogue in Capernaum. A man possessed with a demon says he knows who Jesus is, and Jesus orders him to be quiet and come out. When the demon leaves the man, everyone is amazed. Jesus heals Simon's mother-in-law and in the evening, He continues to heal the sick and drive out demons.

MOLD

Jesus still calls us today. Let us respond to His call like the disciples did: by following Him immediately.

When Jesus called the first disciples, they immediately _____ Him. Go through the maze and write the answer in the box. (verse 18)

The answer key is on page 100.

PRAYER

Dear Jesus, thank you for calling us while we were still sinners. When I hear Your voice, help me to obey immediately like the first disciples did.

21

03

Mark 1:35–45

Not Looking for Fame

* Synagogues are meeting places where the Jews gather to worship God together.

sticker

[35] It was very early in the morning. [...] Jesus [...] went to a place where he could be alone. There he prayed. [36] Simon and his friends went to look for Jesus. [37] When they found him, they called out, "Everyone is looking for you!" [38] Jesus replied, "Let's go [...] to the nearby towns." [...] [39] So he traveled all around Galilee. He preached in their synagogues. He also drove out demons. [40] A man who had a skin disease came. [...] He said, "If you are willing to make me 'clean,' you can do it." [41] [...] "I am willing," [...] Jesus said. "Be 'clean'!" [42] Right away the disease left the man, and he was "clean." [43] Jesus [...] gave the man a strong warning. [44] "Don't tell this to anyone," he said. [...] "Offer the sacrifices that Moses commanded. It will be a witness to the [...] people that you are 'clean.'" [45] But the man went out and started talking right away. [...] So Jesus [...] stayed outside in lonely places. But people still came to him. [...]

MIX

Jesus goes to a quiet place to pray alone. Afterwards, Jesus decides to go to nearby towns to preach, drive out demons, and heal people. Jesus heals a man with a skin disease and tells him to keep quiet about it and to go offer sacrifices as Moses' laws require. However, the man goes out and starts telling people about Jesus' miracle.

MOLD

As followers of Jesus, let us not seek popularity. Instead, let us quietly and faithfully do the good works God prepared in advance for us to do.

BAKE

Write about your day in words and in pictures. Pray to God and express your feelings about the things He has allowed in your day and the lessons you learned from them.

PRAYER

Dear God, thank you for bringing eternal life through Jesus. Help me to quietly and faithfully obey You rather than trying to be popular among my friends.

23

04

Mark 2:1–12

Authority over Sin

PREPARE

* The roofs in Jesus' time were not made of concrete or metal. They were made of hay, wood, and mud, so they were easier to break.

sticker

¹ [..] Jesus entered Capernaum. [..] ² So many people gathered that there was no room left. [..] ³ Four of those who came were carrying a man who could not walk. ⁴ But they could not get him close to Jesus. [..] So they made a hole by digging through the roof above Jesus. Then they lowered the man through it. [..] ⁵ Jesus saw their faith. So he said to the man, "Son, your sins are forgiven." ⁶ Some teachers of the law were [..] thinking, ⁷ [..] "Only God can forgive sins!" ⁸ Right away Jesus knew. [..] So he said to them, [..] ⁹ "Is it easier to say to this man, 'Your sins are forgiven'? Or to say, 'Get up, take your mat and walk'? ¹⁰ But I want you to know that the Son of Man has authority on earth to forgive sins." So Jesus spoke to the man. [..] ¹¹ "I tell you," he said, "get up. Take your mat and go home." ¹² The man got up and took his mat. Then he walked away. [..] All the people were amazed. They praised God. [..]

MIX

Jesus continues teaching. There are so many people that there is no room left. Some friends bring in a man who cannot walk by making a hole in the roof. Jesus sees their faith and tells the man that his sins are forgiven. When He sees what the teachers of the law are thinking, He shows them His authority by healing the man and enabling him to walk.

MOLD Even though we may not say our bad thoughts out loud, Jesus knows and hears all. Let us cultivate thoughts that honor and please Him.

BAKE

Fill in the blanks. The answers can be found in the Bible passage.

When Jesus enters a home in Capernaum, there are so many people that there is no r_____ left. Some friends bring in a man who cannot w_____. They ask Jesus to heal him. Jesus sees their f_____. He forgives his s_____ and heals him. People are a_____ and praise God.

TASTE

Which of the thoughts below would be considered bad? Which would be considered good? Circle the thoughts that are good and pleasing before God.

'I am going to cheat to get a point in this game.'

'I am grateful that God allowed me to be a fast runner.'

'I will not cheat even if it means losing this game.'

'I am better than my friends because I can run faster.'

PRAYER

Dear Jesus, You have the authority to forgive our sins and heal us. You know my deepest thoughts, so help me think of the things that please and honor God the Father.

25

FRI

05

Mark 2:13–20

Coming for the Sinners

PREPARE

* Jewish tax collectors were seen as those who betrayed their own people. They were disowned and disliked by the Jewish.

sticker

13 Once again Jesus went out beside the Sea of Galilee. A large crowd came to him. [...] 14 [...] He saw Levi. [...] Levi was sitting at the tax collector's booth. "Follow me," Jesus told him. Levi [...] followed him. 15 Later Jesus was having dinner at Levi's house. Many tax collectors and sinners were eating with him. [...] 16 Some [...] Pharisees were there. [...] They asked his disciples, "Why does he eat with tax collectors and sinners?" 17 Jesus [...] said to them, "Those who are healthy don't need a doctor. [...] I have not come to get those who think they are right with God to follow me. I have come to get sinners to follow me." 18 [...] Some people [...] said to him, "John's disciples are fasting. [...] But your disciples are not. Why aren't they?" 19 Jesus answered, "How can the guests of the groom go without eating while he is with them? [...] 20 But the time will come when the groom will be taken away from them. On that day they will go without eating."

MIX

A crowd gathers around Jesus. Jesus calls Levi to follow Him. He goes to his house and eats with tax collectors and sinners. The Pharisees ask His disciples why Jesus is doing this. Jesus Himself answers them saying that He has come to get sinners to follow Him. Then some people ask why His disciples do not fast. He tells them that once He is gone, they will.

MOLD

Just as Jesus had compassion upon the people who were rejected, let us have compassion for the less popular people around us.

BAKE

As you read the comic below, think about for whom Jesus came for in this world.

PRAYER

Dear God, thank you for sending Your Son so that a sinner like me could follow You! Help me to show Jesus' compassion to those around me.

27

SAT

06

Mark 2:23–3:6

According to the Law

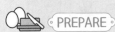

PREPARE

* Only priests were allowed to eat the holy bread.

sticker

23 One Sabbath day Jesus was walking with his disciples through the grainfields. The disciples began to break off some heads of grain. 24 The Pharisees said, [...] "It is against the Law to do this on the Sabbath." [...] 25 He answered, [...] "David [...] and his men were hungry. [...] 26 [...] David entered the house of God and ate the holy bread. [...] 27 [...] The Sabbath day was made for man. [...] 28 So the Son of Man is Lord even of the Sabbath day."

3:1 Another time Jesus went into the synagogue. A man with a [...] twisted hand was there. 2 Some Pharisees [...] wanted to see if he would heal the man on the Sabbath day. [...] 4 [...] Jesus asked them, "What does the Law say we should do on the Sabbath day? Should we do good? Or should we do evil?" [...] No one answered. 5 Jesus [...] was very upset because their hearts were stubborn. Then he said to the man, "Stretch out your hand." [...] His hand had become as good as new. 6 Then the Pharisees [...] began to make plans [...] to kill Jesus.

MIX

On the Sabbath, Jesus' disciples break off heads of grain and eat them. The Pharisees question Jesus about it. Jesus answers by telling them how David and His men ate the holy bread. He tells them the Sabbath was made for man, so He is Lord over it. Jesus heals a man with a twisted hand on another Sabbath. The Pharisees are angry and plot to kill Him.

MOLD

When the Law is not in our hearts, it is easy to misinterpret it like the Pharisees did. Let us ask God to put His Law in our hearts.

BAKE

The Pharisees were upset with Jesus because of how He did or did not do some things on the _____. This was the day God had set apart for the Israelites to rest. (verse 24)

T

H

Start

S

A

A

B

B

The answer key is on page 100.

PRAYER

Dear God, You are Lord over the Sabbath. Help me to rest in You. Please put Your Law in my heart so that I may not sin against You.

WEEK

We memorize things quicker when we write them out. To help you memorize this week's memory verse, write out the Bible verse below.

"Anyone who does what God wants is my brother or sister or mother."

Mark 3:35

"Anyone who does what God wants is my brother or sister or mother."

Mark 3:35

Jesus and His Disciples

07 SUN

PREPARE

* Boanerges means Sons of Thunder.

sticker

7 Jesus went off to the Sea of Galilee with his disciples. A large crowd from Galilee followed. [...] 9 Because of the crowd, Jesus told his disciples to get a small boat ready for him. [...] 10 Jesus had healed many people. So those who were sick were pushing forward to touch him. [...] 13 Jesus [...] called for certain people to come to him, and they came. 14 He appointed 12 of them so that they would be with him. He would also send them out to preach. 15 And he gave them authority to drive out demons. 16 [...] Simon was one of them. Jesus gave him the name Peter. 17 There were James [...] and his brother John. Jesus gave them the name Boanerges. [...] 18 There were also Andrew, Philip, Bartholomew, Matthew, Thomas, and James. [...] And there were Thaddaeus and Simon the Zealot. 19 Judas Iscariot was one of them too. He was the one who was later going to hand Jesus over to his enemies.

MIX

A large crowd continues to follow Jesus near the Sea of Galilee. He heals many and drives out evil spirits. People push forward to try to touch Him. The evil spirits recognize who He is and shout it out. He orders the evil spirits to keep quiet. He then goes to a mountainside and appoints twelve disciples. Among them is Judas Iscariot, who is going to betray Jesus.

MOLD

The fact that we are reading and following Jesus' words in the Bible means that we too are His disciples! Let us rejoice in this and continue following Him.

Family Devotional

This study is designed to take you deeper into today's Bible passage and help your family enjoy the Word of God together. Open with prayer and a song of praise. Share about your week, including answers to prayers and things you are thankful for.

OBSERVE

1. What happens when Jesus withdraws to the lake? (verse 7)

2. What does Jesus do on the shores of the lake? (verse10)

3. Why did Jesus call the twelve? (verses 14–15)

DISCUSS

Discuss the ways God calls people today.

APPLY

What has God called your family to be and to do?

FAMILY PRAYER POINTS

1.

2.

3.

PRAYER

Dear Jesus, thank you for calling us to Yourself. Help us know what pleases You so that we can listen and obey. In Your name, amen.

Part of Jesus' Family

PREPARE

* Teachers of the law from Jerusalem were very important and distinguished because Jerusalem was the Jewish capital.

sticker

20 [...] Again a crowd gathered. [...] Jesus and his disciples were not even able to eat. 21 His family heard about this. [...] 22 Some teachers of the law were there. They had come down from Jerusalem. They said, [...] "He is driving out demons by the power of the prince of demons." 23 So Jesus called them over to him. [...] He said, "How can Satan drive out Satan? [...] 25 If a family is divided, it can't stand. 26 And if Satan fights against himself, and his helpers are divided, he can't stand. [...] 31 Jesus' mother and brothers came and stood outside. They sent someone in to get him. 32 A crowd was sitting around Jesus. They told him, "Your mother and your brothers are outside [...] looking for you." 33 "Who is my mother? Who are my brothers?" he asked. 34 Then Jesus looked at the people sitting [...] around him. He said, "Here is my mother! Here are my brothers! 35 Anyone who does what God wants is my brother or sister or mother."

MIX

The crowd is so big that Jesus does not have time to eat. Some teachers of the law from Jerusalem are there and they think Jesus is driving out demons by the power of Satan. Jesus tells them that if Satan were to fight himself, he would not be able to stand. Jesus' family sends for Him, and Jesus tells the crowd that whoever does what God wants is His family.

MOLD

Whether we are playing with friends, going to school, or eating with our family, let us do what God wants. In all that we do, let us ask what He wants and obey gladly.

BAKE

Whoever does what God wants is considered to be Jesus' _____, sister, or mother. Trace the lines in each box to spell out the correct letters. (verse 35)

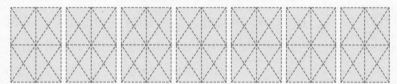

TASTE

As you find **the five hidden items**, do your best to live by God's will as a member of Jesus' true family.

The answer will be uploaded on ILJ Instagram page at the end of the month: *instagram.com/ilovejesus_duranno*

Hidden items: pouch bag, gift box, glove, banana, kettle

PRAYER

Dear Jesus, You call those who do what God wants Your family. As part of Your eternal family, help me to always do what You want and to do it with joy in my heart!

TUE

Mark 4:1–20

Good Soil

09

PREPARE

* Jesus is again teaching a large crowd by the Sea of Galilee.

sticker

¹ Again Jesus [..] ² [..] said, ³ "Listen! A farmer [..] ⁴ [..] scattered [..] seed. [..] Some fell on a path. Birds [..] ate it up. ⁵ Some seed fell on rocky places. [..] ⁶ [..] They dried up because they had no roots. ⁷ Other seed fell among thorns. The thorns [..] crowded out the plants. [..] ⁸ Still other seed fell on good soil. It [..] produced a crop." [..] ¹⁰ [..] The 12 disciples asked him about the stories. [..] ¹¹ He told them, [..] ¹⁴ "The seed [..] is God's message. ¹⁵ What is seed scattered on a path like? [..] The people hear the message. Then Satan [..] takes away the message. [..] ¹⁶ And what is seed scattered on rocky places like? The people hear the message. [..] ¹⁷ But [..] they quickly fall away from the faith when trouble [..] comes. [..] ¹⁸ And what is seed scattered among thorns like? [..] ¹⁹ [..] Worries [..] come. [..] These [..] things [..] keep it from producing fruit. ²⁰ And what is seed scattered on good soil like? The people hear the message. They accept it. They produce a good crop." [..]

MIX

Jesus tells the crowd a a parable. A farmer scatters seeds. Some fall on rocky and thorny grounds and die off. Other seed fall on good soil and produces a crop. He explains the meaning of this to His disciples. The seed is God's message and the rocky and thorny places are troubles or worries that choke and kill the seed. But the seed falling on good soil is when people hear and accept the message.

MOLD

Let us be like the good soil. Let us hear and accept God's message of forgiveness, love, and hope. As we do, we will produce a good crop for God.

BAKE

The seed from the story Jesus told is God's _____. Check the box that spells out the correct answer. (verse 14)

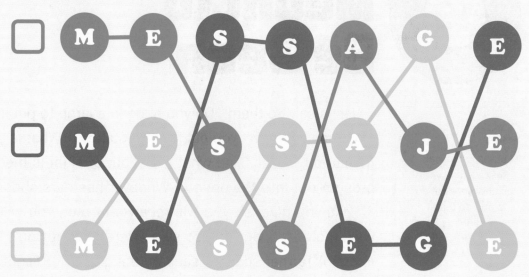

TASTE

Do you think you have been listening to God's Word with all your heart? Examine your mind or attitude as you finish the picture with out lifting your pencil.

START ➡

PRAYER

Dear God, do not allow worries and troubles to kill the Word of God in my heart. Help me be like good soil and produce a good crop for Your glory.

WED

10

Mark 4:21–29

Meant to Be Seen

◦ PREPARE ◦

* Lamps in biblical times were lit with oil and were put on a stand so that it would light as much in the room as possible.

sticker

21 Jesus said to them, "Do you bring in a lamp to put it under a large bowl? [...] Don't you put it on its stand? 22 What is hidden is meant to be seen. And what is put out of sight is meant to be brought out into the open. 23 Whoever has ears should listen. 24 [...] As you give, so you will receive. In fact, you will receive even more." [...] 26 Jesus also said, "Here is what God's kingdom is like. A farmer scatters seed on the ground. 27 Night and day the seed comes up and grows. It happens whether the farmer sleeps or gets up. He doesn't know how it happens. 28 All by itself the soil produces grain. First the stalk comes up. Then the head appears. Finally, the full grain appears in the head. 29 Before long the grain ripens. So the farmer cuts it down, because the harvest is ready."

◦ MIX ◦

Jesus tells the crowd that a lamp is meant to be seen and what is hidden is also meant to be brought out in the open. He also tells them that in giving they will receive more. He then likens God's kingdom to a farmer who scatters seed. The seeds grow until the harvest is ready, whether the farmer is awake or asleep. The farmer simply cuts it down when the harvest is ready.

◦ MOLD ◦

Jesus' parables are not meant to be understood with simple intellect. We are to listen to it with God's heart. So, let us ask the Holy Spirit to reveal more of His kingdom to us.

Write about your day in words and in pictures. Pray to God and express your feelings about the things He has allowed in your day and the lessons you learned from them.

BAKE

PRAYER Dear God, Your kingdom continues to grow according to Your good plans. Give me eyes to see and ears to hear so that I may recognize how You are working in and through me.

11

Mark 4:30–41

Like a Mustard Seed

PREPARE

* The mustard seed is one of the smallest of all seeds on earth.

sticker

³⁰ Again Jesus said, [...] "God's kingdom is [...] ³¹ [...] like a mustard seed. [...] ³² [...] When you plant the seed, it grows. It becomes the largest of all garden plants." [...] ³⁴ He did not say anything to them without using a story. But when he was alone with his disciples, he explained everything. ³⁵ When evening came, Jesus said to his disciples, "Let's go over to the other side of the lake." ³⁶ [...] They took him along in a boat. [...] ³⁷ A wild storm came up. Waves crashed over the boat. It was about to sink. ³⁸ Jesus was [...] sleeping. [...] The disciples [...] said, "Teacher! Don't you care if we drown?" ³⁹ He got up and ordered the wind to stop. He said to the waves, "Quiet! Be still!" [...] And it was completely calm. ⁴⁰ He said to his disciples, "Why are you so afraid? Don't you have any faith?" [...] ⁴¹ [...] They asked each other, "Who is this? Even the wind and the waves obey him!"

MIX

Jesus compares God's kingdom to a mustard seed, that when planted, grows to become very large. Afterwards, Jesus and His disciples get on a boat to go to the other side of the lake. A storm comes up and the boat is about to sink. Jesus is sleeping, so His disciples wake Him up. Jesus orders the wind and waves to calm down and they do.

MOLD

God's kingdom is always growing and expanding. Let us trust God has the authority to calm the winds and waves in our lives and let us continue to seek His expanding kingdom.

BAKE

Jesus likens God's kingdom to a _____ seed, which becomes the largest of garden plants once it grows. Connect the boxes to spell out the answer. (verse 31)

```
M  T  M  D  M     R
 M  E  N  U  U  S  M
U  T  R  S  A  S
 N  S  A  D  N  T  D
A  R  N  S  A  U
```

The answer key is on page 100.

TASTE

Are there any winds, waves, or storms in your life? Write down any difficulties you have before God and put your fears aside as you put your faith in Him.

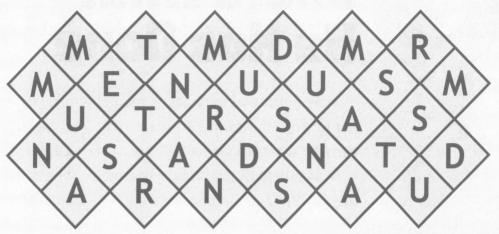

Difficulties in my life: _____

_____

_____

God, I lay these difficulties down before You.

Help me to not be afraid.

PRAYER

Dear God, Your kingdom continues to grow. Help me to trust in Your authority over every difficulty and trial, and help me to seek Your kingdom and righteousness.

41

12

Mark 5:2–20

Share What He Has Done

² Jesus got out of the boat. A man controlled by an evil spirit came from the tombs to meet him. [...] ⁹ [...] Jesus asked the demon, "What is your name?" "My name is Legion," he replied. [...] ¹¹ A large herd of pigs was [...] nearby. [...] ¹² The demons begged Jesus, "Send us among the pigs." [...] ¹³ Jesus allowed it. The

MIX

Jesus meets a man controlled by evil spirits. When Jesus confronts the evil spirits, they ask to be sent to the pigs and Jesus allows it. The evil spirits go into the pigs and they drown in the lake. The townspeople hear about this and are afraid. They ask Him to leave. Jesus tells the man who had been controlled by demons to stay and tell others about Him.

MOLD

Without Jesus, our lives are controlled by something that is not from God. Let us ask Jesus to take control of our lives and be ready to share how much He has done for us.

evil spirits came out of the man and went into the pigs. [...] The whole herd [...] ran into the lake and drowned. 14 Those who were tending the pigs [...] told the people in the town. [...] 15 [...] All this made the people afraid. [...] 17 Then the people began to beg Jesus to leave. [...] 18 Jesus was getting into the boat. The man who had been controlled by demons begged to go with him. 19 Jesus [...] said, "Go home to your own people. Tell them how much the Lord has done for you." [...] 20 So [...] he began to tell how much Jesus had done for him. And all the people were amazed.

 PREPARE

* The pigs that the evil spirits went into were about 2,000 in number.

sticker

PRAYER
Dear God, You have done and continue to do so much good in my life. Thank you for this. Help me to share about what You have done in my life with others.

Just Believe

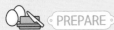

* Jairus was a syna-
gogue leader.

sticker

²¹ Jesus went across the Sea of Galilee. [...] ²² Then a man named Jairus [...] ²³ [...] begged Jesus, [...] "My little daughter is dying. [...] Heal her." [...] ²⁴ So Jesus went with him. A large group [...] followed. [...] ²⁵ A woman was there who had a sickness that made her bleed. [...] ²⁷ [...] She [...] touched his clothes. ²⁸ She thought, "I just need to touch his clothes. Then I will be healed." ²⁹ [...] Her bleeding stopped. [...] ³⁰ [...] Jesus [...] asked, "Who touched my clothes?" [...] ³³ Then the woman came and [...] `told him. [...] ³⁴ He said to her, [...] "Your faith has healed you. Go in peace." [...] ³⁵ [...] Some people came from the house of Jairus. [...] "Your daughter is dead," they said. [...] ³⁶ Jesus [...] told the synagogue leader, [...] "Just believe." [...] ⁴⁰ [...] He went in where the child was. ⁴¹ He took her by the hand. Then he said to her, "Talitha koum!" This means, "Little girl, I say to you, get up!" ⁴² [...] She stood up. [...] ⁴³ Jesus gave strict orders not to let anyone know what had happened. [...]

MIX

Jairus asks Jesus to come heal his daughter. A large crowd follows Him. Among them is a very sick woman. She touches His clothes thinking this would heal her. Jesus tells her it is her faith that healed her. Meanwhile, Jairus is told his daughter died. Jesus still goes to his house and encourages Jairus to believe. Once there, He tells the girl to get up and she does.

MOLD

Believing God is what is required of us as believers. Let us put our wholehearted faith in God in every area of our lives.

Jesus tells the bleeding woman that it is her faith that healed her. Then, he wishes her to ___ ___ _____. (verse 34)

What are some things about God that you believe? Write them down below.

I believe God _____.

_____

_____

_____

_____

Dear God, You are the Healer that heals our physical and spiritual illness. Help me to wholeheartedly believe in You at all times.

45

WEEK

We memorize things quicker when we write them out. To help you memorize this week's memory verse, write out the Bible verse below.

"It is what comes
out of them that
makes them 'unclean.' "

Mark 7:15–16

"It is what comes
out of them that
makes them 'unclean.' "

Mark 7:15–16

14

Let Us Receive Jesus

 PREPARE

* Jesus' hometown
  is Nazareth.

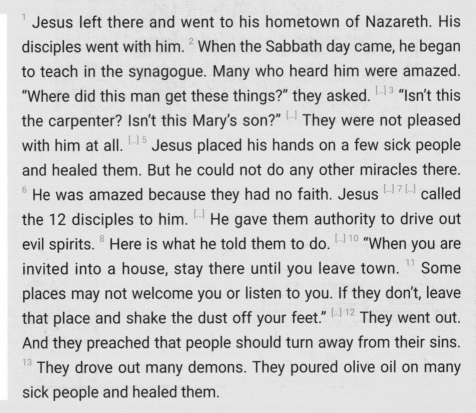

sticker

¹ Jesus left there and went to his hometown of Nazareth. His disciples went with him. ² When the Sabbath day came, he began to teach in the synagogue. Many who heard him were amazed. "Where did this man get these things?" they asked. [...] ³ "Isn't this the carpenter? Isn't this Mary's son?" [...] They were not pleased with him at all. [...] ⁵ Jesus placed his hands on a few sick people and healed them. But he could not do any other miracles there. ⁶ He was amazed because they had no faith. Jesus [...] ⁷ [...] called the 12 disciples to him. [...] He gave them authority to drive out evil spirits. ⁸ Here is what he told them to do. [...] ¹⁰ "When you are invited into a house, stay there until you leave town. ¹¹ Some places may not welcome you or listen to you. If they don't, leave that place and shake the dust off your feet." [...] ¹² They went out. And they preached that people should turn away from their sins. ¹³ They drove out many demons. They poured olive oil on many sick people and healed them.

 MIX

Jesus teaches at a synagogue in Nazareth. People are amazed but dislike His teaching because they know Him as the local carpenter's son. Jesus says He knew He would not be honored there. He sends His disciples out and gives them specific instructions of what to do and not do. Thus, they preach, drive out demons, and heal many sick people.

 MOLD

Jesus was rejected even though He spoke words of life. Let us also boldly speak what God puts in our hearts and not be surprised if we face rejection.

Family Devotional

This study is designed to take you deeper into today's Bible passage and help your family enjoy the Word of God together. Open with prayer and a song of praise. Share about your week, including answers to prayers and things you are thankful for.

OBSERVE

1. How do the people in Jesus' hometown respond to His teaching? (verses 2–3)

2. What authority did Jesus give to His twelve disciples? (verse 7)

3. What do the disciples do once they are sent out? (verses 12–13)

DISCUSS

How do people respond to Jesus today? Discuss reasons for their response.

APPLY

How can you welcome Jesus into your everyday life as a family?

FAMILY PRAYER POINTS

1.

2.

3.

PRAYER

Dear Jesus, thank you for enabling us to receive Your truth and love. Help us spread the gospel to those around us as Your faithful disciples without fear of rejection. In Your name, amen.

MON

15

Mark 6:14–29

Be Careful with Promises

PREPARE

* Herodias was the wife of Herod's brother Philip. But now Herod was married to her.

sticker

14 King Herod heard about this. [...] 16 [...] Herod [...] said, [...] "John [...] has been raised from the dead!" 17 [...] It was Herod himself who had given orders to arrest John. [...] 18 John had been saying to Herod, "It is against the Law for you to be married to your brother's wife." [...] 20 [...] Herod was afraid of John. So he kept John safe. [...] 21 Finally the right time came. Herod gave a banquet. [...] 22 [...] The daughter of Herodias [...] danced. She pleased Herod. [...] The king said, [...] "Ask me for anything." [...] 24 She [...] said to her mother, "What should I ask for?" "The head of John," [...] she answered. 25 [...] The girl [...] said, "I want you to give me the head of John the Baptist." [...] 27 He sent a man [...] to bring John's head. The man [...] cut off John's head. 28 He brought it back. [...] 29 John's disciples heard [...] and took his body. Then they placed it in a tomb.

MIX

Herod hears about Jesus and thinks He could be John raised from the dead. He thinks back on how he had arrested John because he had spoken against his marriage to Herodias. During a banquet, he had told Herodias' daughter that he would grant her any wish. After consulting with her mother, she asked for John's head on a platter. He granted the request and killed John.

50

MOLD

Let us be careful and not make careless promises that could make us do something we know to be wrong.

BAKE

There are times we may be tempted to do or say things in order to be liked and accepted by our friends. However, we should be careful to not tie ourselves to do something that displeases God in order to gain "friends." As you read the comic below, consider what is the right way of acting.

We should not make promises that could lead to sin.

We should love our friends but refrain from bad promises.

PRAYER

Dear God, help me to be mindful of the promises I make. Help me to not say something that could lead me to do something that is sinful or wrong.

Mark 6:34–44

All of Them Were Satisfied

○ PREPARE ○

* In the Old Testament, God fed the Israelites with manna and quail while they were in the wilderness. Here, Jesus feeds the people with bread and fish.

sticker

34 When Jesus came ashore, he saw a large crowd. He felt deep concern for them. They were like sheep without a shepherd. So he began teaching them many things. 35 By that time it was late in the day. His disciples came to him. [...] 36 "Send the people away. Then they can go [...] and [...] buy something to eat." [...] 38 "How many loaves do you have?" Jesus asked. [...] When they found out, they said, "Five loaves and two fish." [...] 41 Jesus took the five loaves and the two fish. He looked up to heaven and gave thanks. He broke the loaves into pieces. Then he gave them to his disciples to pass around to the people. He also divided the two fish among them all. 42 All of them ate and were satisfied. 43 The disciples picked up 12 baskets of broken pieces of bread and fish. 44 The number of men who had eaten was 5,000.

○ MIX ○

Seeing the large crowd that is following Him, Jesus has compassion for them and begins to teach them. As it gets late, the disciples want to dismiss them, but Jesus tells them to feed the crowd. The doubting disciples bring five loaves and two fish, but Jesus multiplies this to feed over 5,000 people. Everyone eats and is satisfied.

○ MOLD ○

Nothing in this world could satisfy us like Jesus, who provides for us everything we need. Let us thank Him for not only giving us things to eat but also satisfying our souls with His abundant love.

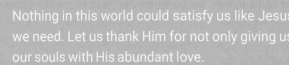

As you read the comic below, give thanks to God for His generosity and ask Him to give you a loving heart, so that you can share what you have with others.

Dear God, my soul is empty and hungry after chasing after the things of the world. Give me Jesus, for only He can satisfy my soul with His peace and grace.

WED

17

Mark 6:45–56

Be Brave!

○ PREPARE ○

* In the Old Testament, God led the Israelites through the Red Sea. Here, Jesus leads the disciples through a windy lake, showing His power as God's Son.

sticker

[45] Right away Jesus made his disciples get into the boat. He had them go on ahead of him to Bethsaida. Then he sent the crowd away. [46] [...] He went up on a mountainside to pray. [47] Later that night, the boat was in the middle of the Sea of Galilee. Jesus was alone on land. [48] He saw the disciples pulling hard on the oars. The wind was blowing against them. Shortly before dawn, he went out to them. He walked on the lake. When he was about to pass by them, [49] they saw him walking on the lake. They thought he was a ghost, so they [...] [50] [...] were terrified. [...] Jesus said to them, "Be brave! It is I." [...] [51] Then he climbed into the boat with them. The wind died down. [...] [52] They had not understood about the loaves. They were stubborn. [53] They [...] landed at Gennesaret. [...] [56] [...] Everywhere he went, the people [...] were healed.

○ MIX ○

After feeding 5,000 people, Jesus sends His disciples ahead of Him to Bethsaida. While they are crossing the lake, a violent wind blows against them. Jesus comes to them, walking on the lake. After Jesus makes the wind die down, the disciples are greatly amazed. They still do not realize that He is the Son of God, even after Jesus performed the miracle of feeding 5,000 people.

○ MOLD ○

Let us be brave in whatever situation because Jesus is always with us in our trouble and gives us His peace.

BAKE

Write about your day in words and in pictures. Pray to God and express your feelings about the things He has allowed in your day and the lessons you learned from them.

15
+18

PRAYER

Dear God, when I find myself in a difficult situation, my heart trembles like a windy lake. Let Jesus come to me in my troubles and give me peace.

18

Mark 7:1–13

Making God's Word Useless

PREPARE

* Corban refers to a practice among the Jewish people of making a vow or dedicating something as a gift to God.

sticker

[1] The Pharisees [...] [2] [...] saw some of his disciples eating food with "unclean" hands. [...] [5] So the Pharisees [...] questioned Jesus. "Why don't your disciples live by what the elders teach?" they asked. [...] [6] He replied, "Isaiah [...] prophesied about you people who pretend to be good. He said, 'These people honor me by what they say. But their hearts are far away from me.' [...] [8] You have let go of God's commands. And you are holding on to teachings that people have made up." [...] [10] Moses said, 'Honor your father and mother.' [...] [11] But you allow people to say that what might have been used to help their parents is Corban. [...] [13] You make the word of God useless by putting your own teachings in its place. And you do many things like this."

MIX

The Jewish religious leaders, who had a special law about washing, ask Jesus why His disciples eat food without washing their hands first. They thought that this makes a person religiously unclean. However, Jesus tells them that while they act religiously, their hearts are far from God. This is because they make religious laws of their own and use them as an excuse to not follow God's Word.

MOLD

Let us not make laws of our own above God's Word. Following our own laws that go above God's Word means that our hearts are far from God.

BAKE

Isaiah prophesied about the Pharisees when he said that some would honor God by what they said, but their _____ would be far away from Him. (verse 6)

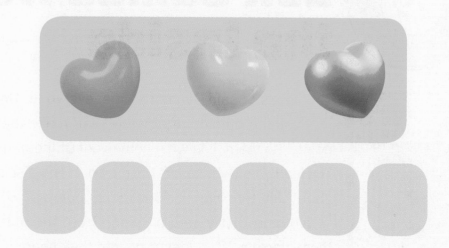

TASTE

For which of the following reasons was Jesus not pleased with the Pharisees? Circle the ones that are correct.

1 Because they helped people in need.

2 Because they cherished God's words and tried to live by them.

3 Because they were holding on to teachings that people made above God's words.

4 Because they honored God only by what they said.

PRAYER

Dear God, if I made and followed my own rules above Your Word, forgive me and help me let go of them. I want to be close to You by following Your Word.

FRI

19

Mark 7:14–22

Evil Comes from the Inside

 PREPARE

* Heart here does not mean the physical organ, but the inner being of a person, where our feelings and thoughts come from.

sticker

¹⁴ [..] Jesus [..] said, "Listen to me, everyone. Understand this. ¹⁵⁻¹⁶ Nothing outside of a person can make them 'unclean' by going into them. It is what comes out of them that makes them 'unclean.' " ¹⁷ Then he left the crowd. [..] His disciples asked him about this teaching. ¹⁸ "Don't you understand?" Jesus asked. [..] "Nothing that enters a person from the outside can make them 'unclean.' ¹⁹ It doesn't go into their heart. It goes into their stomach." [..] In saying this, Jesus was calling all foods "clean." ²⁰ He went on to say, "What comes out of a person is what makes them 'unclean.' ²¹ Evil thoughts come from the inside, from a person's heart. [..] ²² [..] And so do telling lies about others and being proud and being foolish."

 MIX

The Pharisees taught the people that outward things, such as not washing one's hands, make a person unclean. However, Jesus teaches that what truly makes a person unclean are the evil thoughts and feelings that come out of a person's heart. Out of a sinful heart comes evil thoughts and feelings such as adultery and hate, and they lead to evil actions such as stealing.

58

 MOLD

Because God looks at the heart, we should focus on keeping our heart clean. Let us ask Jesus to wash our sins away and to keep us holy through His Holy Spirit.

Fill in the blanks with the letter that matches each picture from the box below to reveal the message.

BAKE

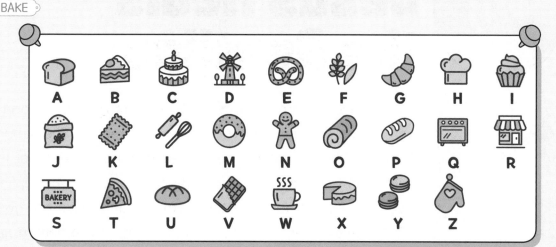

A B C D E F G H I
J K L M N O P Q R
S T U V W X Y Z

ASK GOD TO REMOVE

SINFUL THOUGHTS

AND MAKE YOUR

HEART CLEAN.

Dear God, I know I am a sinner because evil thoughts come out of my heart. Wash my sins away in Jesus' name and help me to follow Your holy Word.

PRAYER

(20)

Mark 7:24–35

Jesus Heals the Gentiles

(PREPARE)

* Tyre is a coastal city in the Gentile (non-Jewish) territory. Jesus is expanding His ministry beyond the Jewish regions to the Gentile regions.

sticker

24 Jesus went from there to a place near Tyre. [...] 25 Soon a woman heard about him. [...] 26 She was a Greek. [...] She *begged* Jesus to drive the *demon* out of her daughter. 27 "First let the children eat all they want," he told her. [...] 28 "Lord," she replied, "even the dogs under the table eat the children's crumbs." 29 Then he told her, "That was a good reply. [...] The demon has left your daughter." [...] 31 Then Jesus [...] went [...] into the area known as the Ten Cities. 32 There some people brought a man to Jesus. The man was *deaf* and could hardly speak. [...] 33 Jesus [...] put his fingers into the man's ears [...] and touched the man's *tongue*. 34 Jesus looked up to *heaven*. [...] He said to the man, "Ephphatha!" That means "Be opened!" 35 The man's ears were *opened*. His tongue was freed up. [...]

(MIX)

A Greek woman approaches Jesus, asking Him to heal her daughter who is controlled by an evil spirit. Although Jesus tells her that He has to first feed the Israelites, the woman responds that even dogs eat the crumbs that fall from the table. Seeing her faith, Jesus heals her daughter. Jesus then heals a man who is both mute and deaf.

(MOLD)

Jesus, as the Son of God, not only has the power to heal His creation but has compassion for all people. Let us imitate Him and have compassion for all the people around us.

BAKE

Find the words written in a different font from today's Scripture in the word search below.

K	F	M	V	T	R	O	B	H	X
Y	I	O	P	E	N	E	D	S	Z
D	E	A	F	H	T	W	K	V	U
L	Y	Z	C	R	E	D	U	E	J
T	O	K	T	U	E	A	D	Q	D
O	N	S	F	G	D	J	V	W	H
T	O	N	G	U	E	E	W	E	U
D	J	E	B	J	J	G	M	R	N
J	B	P	I	R	O	D	K	O	F
A	O	O	K	Q	N	N	X	S	N

The answer key is on page 101.

PRAYER

Dear God, thank you for being a compassionate Father to me. Bring healing to my spiritual and physical illnesses and open my eyes and heart to see and love You more.

WEEK

4

We memorize things quicker when we write them out. To help you memorize this week's memory verse, write out the Bible verse below.

"Whoever wants to save their life will lose it. But whoever loses their life for me and for the good news will save it."

Mark 8:35

"Whoever wants to save their life will lose it. But whoever loses their life for me and for the good news will save it."

Mark 8:35

Jesus Can Handle It

21 SUN

 PREPARE

* When Jesus fed 5,000 people, most of them were Jews. This time, when Jesus feeds the 4,000, many are Gentiles. Jesus has compassion on all peoples.

sticker

1 [...] Another large crowd gathered. They had nothing to eat. [...] Jesus [...] said, 2 "I feel deep concern for these people. [...] 3 If I send them away hungry, they will become too weak on their way home." [...] 4 His disciples answered him. "There is nothing here," they said. "Where can anyone get enough bread to feed them?" 5 "How many loaves do you have?" Jesus asked. "Seven," they replied. 6 He told the crowd to sit down on the ground. He took the seven loaves and gave thanks to God. [...] 7 The disciples also had a few small fish. Jesus gave thanks for them too. He told the disciples to pass them around. 8 The people ate and were satisfied. After that, the disciples picked up seven baskets of leftover pieces. 9 About 4,000 people were there. [...] 11 The Pharisees came and began to ask Jesus questions [...] to test him. So they asked him for a sign from heaven. 12 He sighed deeply. He said, "Why do you people ask for a sign? What I'm about to tell you is true." [...] 13 Then he left them. [...]

 MIX

A large crowd followed Jesus and was with Him for three days. Even after seeing Jesus feed 5,000 people, the disciples doubt whether this crowd could be fed. Once again, Jesus feeds the large crowd of 4,000 people with seven loaves of bread and a few fish. However, even after seeing this miracle, the Pharisees do not believe in Jesus and ask Him for other signs.

 MOLD

Jesus showed enough miracles for us to believe in Him as the Son of God. So let us wholeheartedly put our faith in Him.

Family Devotional

This study is designed to take you deeper into today's Bible passage and help your family enjoy the Word of God together. Open with prayer and a song of praise. Share about your week, including answers to prayers and things you are thankful for.

OBSERVE

1. How do the disciples respond when Jesus shows concern for the hungry crowd? (verse 4)

2. What does Jesus do with the seven loaves and few fish the disciples bring to Him? (verses 6–7)

3. What does Jesus do when the Pharisees ask Him for a sign from heaven? (verses 11–13)

DISCUSS

Share how you react to situations that seem too big for you to handle.

APPLY

Share ways in which your family can practice trusting God, especially in situations outside your control.

FAMILY PRAYER POINTS

1.

2.

3.

PRAYER

Dear Jesus, thank you for taking good care of us. Help us to trust You as a family, especially when things do not go as expected. In Your name, amen.

Can You Not Understand Yet?

 PREPARE

* The yeast of the Pharisees and Herod means unbelief. A little bit of yeast makes lots of dough rise as bread. Unbelief could spread like this.

sticker

¹⁴ The disciples had forgotten to bring bread. They had only one loaf with them in the boat. ¹⁵ "Be careful," Jesus warned them. "Watch out for the yeast of the Pharisees. And watch out for the yeast of Herod." ¹⁶ [...] They said, "He must be saying this because we don't have any bread." ¹⁷ Jesus [...] asked them, [...] "Why can't you see or understand? [...] ¹⁹ Earlier I broke five loaves for the 5,000. [...] ²⁰ Later I broke seven loaves for the 4,000. [...] ²¹ [...] Can't you understand yet?" ²² Jesus and his disciples came to Bethsaida. Some people brought a blind man to him. [...] ²³ [...] He [...] placed his hands on him. [...] ²⁴ The man looked up. He said, "I see people. They look like trees walking around." ²⁵ Once more Jesus put his hands on the man's eyes. Then his eyes were opened. [...] He saw everything clearly.

 MIX

While the disciples are concerned with bread, Jesus warns them against a greater danger, which is unbelief. Just like the Pharisees and Herod trust in other things than Jesus, the disciples are in danger of trusting in other things Jesus reminds them of His miracles so that they could put their trust in Him again. Jesus then heals a blind man in two stages.

 MOLD

We are blind and cannot see Jesus if we trust in things other than Him. Let us ask Jesus to open our eyes to see Him, however many stages it takes to heal our unbelief.

BAKE

When the man's sight was partially healed, he told Jesus that he sees people, who look like _____ walking around. Connect the letters to spell out the correct answer. (verse 24)

S	S	T	O	W	O	O	D	S	T	O	R
E											W
R											E
T											W
E											O
E											O
S	E	E	R	T	E	R	R	E	T	S	O

TASTE

If we trust in other things more than we trust in Jesus, we become spiritually blind and deaf. What things are we trusting more than Jesus? Write them below and ask Jesus to heal your spiritual blindness so that you may to see and trust Him.

Trusting in my own intelligence

PRAYER

Dear God, forgive me for being blind and trusting in other things more than in You. Heal my spiritual blindness and help me see You clearly so that I can trust You.

Mark 8:27–35

Pick Up Your Cross

PREPARE

* To pick up one's cross and follow Jesus means to endure suffering for one's faith.

sticker

27 Jesus and his disciples went on to the villages around Caesarea Philippi. On the way he asked them, [...] 29 [...] "Who do you say I am?" Peter answered, "You are the Messiah." [...] 31 Jesus then [...] taught them that the Son of Man must suffer many things. [...] He must be killed and after three days rise again. 32 [...] Peter [...] began to scold him. 33 Jesus [...] scolded Peter. "Get behind me, Satan!" he said. "You are [...] thinking only about the things humans care about." 34 Jesus called the crowd to him along with his disciples. He said, "Whoever wants to be my disciple must say no to themselves. They must pick up their cross and follow me. 35 Whoever wants to save their life will lose it. But whoever loses their life for me and for the good news will save it."

MIX

When Jesus asks His disciples who they think He is, Peter confesses that Jesus is the Messiah. Jesus says that He must suffer, die, and resurrect, but Peter is surprised and tries to scold Jesus. However, Jesus scolds Peter instead and teaches that His followers must suffer for Him. Disciples who are willing to give up their lives for Jesus will gain eternal life.

MOLD

Let us follow Jesus — not only believing in Him as the Messiah but also by being willing to suffer for Him and give up things in this life for Him.

BAKE

Although Peter confesses Jesus as the Messiah, he does not want Jesus to die. However, Jesus tells Peter to get _____ Him, because Jesus must die for our sins. Write the letters by filling in the boxes. (verse 33)

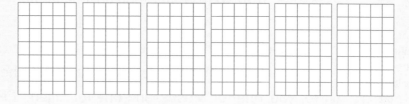

TASTE

Is there anything you need get rid of to become a Jesus' disciple? Think about it and throw them into the garbage can.

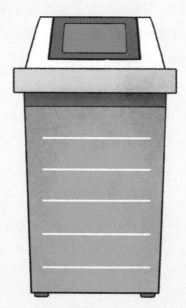

PRAYER

Dear God, forgive me for trying to believe in You without any suffering. Help me to follow You with all my heart, even if the path is laid with suffering.

69

24

Mark 9:2–8

His Changed Appearance

 PREPARE

* The change of Jesus' appearance happens six days after Peter confesses Jesus as Messiah. By changing in appearance, Jesus shows His glory as the Son of God.

sticker

2 After six days Jesus took Peter, James and John with him. He led them up a high mountain. [...] There in front of them his appearance was changed. 3 His clothes became so white they shone. They were whiter than anyone in the world could bleach them. 4 Elijah and Moses appeared in front of Jesus and his disciples. The two of them were talking with Jesus. 5 Peter said to Jesus, "Rabbi, [...] let us put up three shelters. One will be for you, one for Moses, and one for Elijah." 6 Peter didn't really know what to say, because they were so afraid. 7 Then a cloud appeared and covered them. A voice came from the cloud. It said, "This is my Son, and I love him. Listen to him!" 8 They looked around. Suddenly they no longer saw anyone with them except Jesus.

MIX

Six days after Peter confessed Jesus as the Messiah, Jesus takes Peter, James, and John to a high mountain. There, Jesus' appearance changes as his clothes shine brightly, and Elijah and Moses appear next to Him. Peter wants to build three shelters for them, but God tells them to listen to Jesus, His beloved Son. When they look around once more, they see no one except Jesus.

MOLD

Jesus is the glorious Son of God, who fulfills all the promises of the prophets and the law. Therefore, let us listen to Jesus and follow Him.

BAKE

Write about your day in words and in pictures. Pray to God and express your feelings about the things He has allowed in your day and the lessons you learned from them.

15
+18

PRAYER

Dear God, thank you for sending Jesus. Born in a manger, He is the glorious Son of God who came to save me. Help me believe and follow Him.

THU

25

Mark 9:14–29

Overcoming Unbelief!

PREPARE

* A teacher of the law is a religious expert who knows Scripture well and teaches people about it.

sticker

¹⁴ When Jesus [..] came to the other disciples, [..] the teachers of the law were arguing with them. [..] ¹⁶ "What are you arguing with them about?" Jesus asked. ¹⁷ A man in the crowd answered. "Teacher, [..] my son [..] is controlled by an evil spirit. [..] ¹⁸ [..] I asked your disciples to drive out the spirit. But they couldn't do it." [..] ²¹ Jesus asked the boy's father, "How long has he been like this?" "Since he was a child," he answered. ²³ " 'If you can'?" said Jesus. "Everything is possible for the one who believes." ²⁴ Right away the boy's father cried out, "I do believe! Help me overcome my unbelief!" [..] ²⁵ Jesus [..] ordered the evil spirit to leave the boy. [..] ²⁶ The spirit screamed. [..] Then it came out of him. [..] ²⁸ Then his disciples asked him, [..] "Why couldn't we drive out the evil spirit?" ²⁹ He replied, "This kind can come out only by prayer."

MIX

A boy is possessed by an evil spirit, but the disciples cannot drive it out and argue with the teachers of the law about it. When Jesus arrives, the boy's father tells Jesus about his condition and asks Him to help him have faith. After Jesus drives out the evil spirit, the disciples ask why they could not do it. Jesus tells them that such evil spirits come out only by prayer.

MOLD

When evil spirits or thoughts try to attack us in various ways, we need to trust in Jesus and prepare ourselves through prayer.

BAKE

What did the boy's father shout to Jesus, when he doubted yet wanted to trust in Jesus? Place a check mark next to the answer with the correct spelling. (verse 24)

- I DO BELIEVE! HELP MA OVERCOME MY UNBELIEF! ☐
- I DO BELIEVE! HELP ME OBERCOME MY UNBELIEF! ☐
- I DO BELIEVE! HELP ME OVERCOME MY UNBELIEF! ☐
- I DO BELIEVE! HELP ME OVERCAME MY UNBELIEF! ☐
- I DO BELIEVE! HELP ME OVERCOME MY ENBELIEF! ☐

TASTE

Do you believe in the power of prayer? Write a prayer for your home, school, and church, and pray for each topic in faith.

PRAYER

Dear God, help me to overcome my unbelief and trust in You. Help me to pray so that I am prepared to counter act any spiritual attack.

Mark 9:30-37

The First Must Be Last

[30 [..]] Jesus [..] [31 [..]] was teaching his disciples. He said to them, "The Son of Man is going to be handed over to men. They will kill him. After three days he will rise from the dead." [32] But they didn't understand what he meant. [..] [33] Jesus and his disciples came to [.] Capernaum. There he asked them, "What were

Jesus prophesies about His coming death and resurrection, but the disciples do not understand. When Jesus asks the disciples what they were arguing about, they stay silent because they were arguing about who is the greatest among them. However, Jesus tells them that in heaven, the humblest person will be the greatest. He also tells them that welcoming children in His name is the same thing as welcoming God.

MIX

Let us be humble and serve others rather than seeking to be served.

MOLD

74

you arguing about on the road?" [34] But they kept quiet. On the way, they had argued about which one of them was the most important person. [35] Jesus sat down and called for the 12 disciples to come to him. Then he said, "Anyone who wants to be first must be the very last. They must be the servant of everyone." [36] Jesus took a little child [...] in his arms. He said to them, [37] "Anyone who welcomes one of these little children in my name welcomes me. And anyone who welcomes me also welcomes the one who sent me."

 PREPARE

* Capernaum is a town where Jesus does many miracles and teaches His friends. It is like His second home while He lives on earth.

sticker

PRAYER

Dear God, thank you for welcoming a sinner like me. Help me to be like You, so that I can enjoy serving others and welcome those who are left out.

What are you arguing about?

Anyone who wants to be first must be the very last. They must be the servant of everyone.

Anyone who welcomes one of these little children in My name welcomes Me.

If Your Eye Causes you to Sin

* As salt is used to preserve food, to "have salt among yourselves" means to preserve relationships with peace and harmony.

sticker

38 "Teacher," said John, "we saw someone driving out demons in your name. We told him to stop, because he was not one of us." 39 "Do not stop him," Jesus said. [...] 40 "Anyone who is not against us is for us. 41 [...] Suppose someone gives you a cup of water in my name because you belong to the Messiah. That person will certainly not go without a reward. [...] 47 If your eye causes you to sin, poke it out. It would be better for you to enter God's kingdom with only one eye than to have two eyes and be thrown into hell. [...] 50 Salt is good. But suppose it loses its saltiness. How can you make it salty again? Have salt among yourselves. And be at peace with each other."

MIX

The disciples try to stop someone from driving out demons in Jesus' name. Jesus says that anyone who is not against them is for them. Anything good done in Jesus' name will be rewarded. However, anyone who makes a weak Christian fall into sin will be judged by God. Jesus says to cut off whatever leads to sin and to be at peace with others.

MOLD

Let us focus on being at peace among ourselves and fight against sin and anything that leads to sin.

We should be careful of what we look at, because Jesus says that it is better to enter God's _____ without one eye than to enter hell with two eyes. Follow the lines and connect the letters to spell out the correct answer. (verse 47)

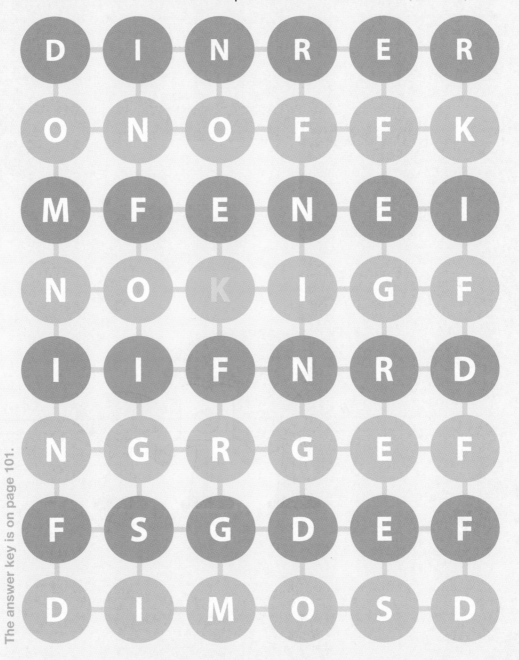

The answer key is on page 101.

D	I	N	R	E	R
O	N	O	F	F	K
M	F	E	N	E	I
N	O	K	I	G	F
I	I	F	N	R	D
N	G	R	G	E	F
F	S	G	D	E	F
D	I	M	O	S	D

PRAYER

Dear God, let me focus on the right things. Help me not to fight against others but rather fight against sin.

WEEK

5

We memorize things quicker when we write them out. To help you memorize this week's memory verse, write out the Bible verse below.

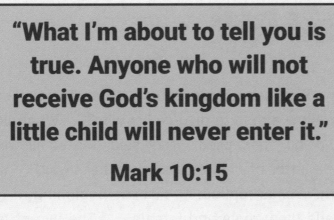

"What I'm about to tell you is true. Anyone who will not receive God's kingdom like a little child will never enter it."

Mark 10:15

"What I'm about to tell you is true. Anyone who will not receive God's kingdom like a little child will never enter it."

Mark 10:15

Mark 10:2–16

God's Good Gift

28 SUN

PREPARE

* To test Jesus means to not trust Him and ask questions with the intention to see Him fail.

sticker

[...] 2 Some Pharisees came to test Jesus. They asked, "Does the Law allow a man to divorce his wife?" 3 "What did Moses command you?" he replied. 4 They said, "Moses allowed a man to write a letter of divorce and send her away." 5 "You were stubborn." Jesus replied. 6 [...] "At the beginning of creation, God 'made them male and female. [...] 8 The two of them will become one.' They are no longer two, but one. 9 So no one should separate what God has joined together." [...] 13 People were bringing little children to Jesus. They wanted him to place his hands on them to bless them. But the disciples told them to stop. 14 Jesus [...] said to his disciples, "Let the little children come to me. [...] God's kingdom belongs to people like them. 15 What I'm about to tell you is true. Anyone who will not receive God's kingdom like a little child will never enter it." 16 Then he took the children in his arms. He placed his hands on them to bless them.

MIX

The Pharisees come to test Jesus, asking Him whether the law of Moses allows a person to divorce. Jesus admits that the law allows divorce, but this was only because people were sinful and stubborn. Jesus teaches that God's will for man and woman was for them to become one without divorce. Jesus tells His dusciples that they should accept God's kingdom like children.

MOLD

Let us not test Jesus as the Pharisees did, but rather accept and follow all of Jesus' teachings about God's kingdom like children.

Family Devotional

This study is designed to take you deeper into today's Bible passage and help your family enjoy the Word of God together. Open with prayer and a song of praise. Share about your week, including answers to prayers and things you are thankful for.

OBSERVE

1. How does Jesus answer the Pharisees' question about divorce? (verses 3–9)

2. What do the disciples do when parents try to bring their children to Jesus? (verse 13)

3. What does Jesus tell His disciples about children? (verses 14–15) How does He respond to the children? (verse 16)

DISCUSS

Describe ways in which little children receive things. How do they respond to gifts?

APPLY

Discuss ways your family can encourage one another to be grateful for God's gift of His kingdom.

FAMILY PRAYER POINTS

1.

2.

3.

PRAYER

Dear Jesus, thank you for welcoming us into Your kingdom and giving us eternal life. Help us always to encourage each other to enjoy Your gift and be grateful for it. In Your name, amen.

29

Mark 10:17–27

Possible with God

 PREPARE

* The commandments Jesus mentions are the Ten Commandments. He first mentions commandments related to loving others, then those related to loving God.

sticker

17 [...] A man ran up to [...] Jesus. [...] "What must I do to receive eternal life?" 18 [...] Jesus answered. "No one is good except God. 19 You know what the commandments say." [...] 20 "Teacher," he said, "I have obeyed all those commandments." [...] 21 Jesus [...] loved him. "You are missing one thing. [...] Sell everything you have. Give the money to those who are poor. You will have treasure in heaven. Then come and follow me." 22 The man [...] went away sad, because he was very rich. 23 Jesus [...] said to his disciples, "How hard it is for rich people to enter God's kingdom!" 24 The disciples were amazed at his words. [...] 27 Jesus [...] said, "With people, this is impossible. But not with God. All things are possible with God."

MIX

When a young rich man comes to Jesus asking how to gain salvation, Jesus tells him the commandments related to loving others. But when the young man says he obeyed all these commandments, Jesus tells him to sell everything and follow Jesus. Hearing this, the man sadly turns back. Jesus says it is hard for rich people to enter heaven, but with God it is possible.

MOLD

Salvation is not possible by human strength but only by God's power. As He saves us, He makes us obedient to His Law. Therefore, let us love God above everything and love others.

Fill in the blanks of the Bible passage using the words provided.

BAKE

commandments	follow
sad	everything
poor	eternal

One day a young man came to Jesus and asked Him, "What should I do to gain _____ life?" Jesus told him obey the _____. When the man told Jesus that he did all these things, Jesus told him to sell _____ and give the money to those who are _____, and to _____ Him. However, the man loved his riches so much, he went away _____.

PRAYER

Dear God, forgive me for making things that You have created into idols. I cast them aside because I love you above all else.

83

30

Mark 10:32–45

Even Jesus Came to Serve

PREPARE

* Sitting at the right and left hand of the throne means having great authority and power next to the king.

sticker

32 They were on their way up to Jerusalem. Jesus [...] told them what was going to happen to him. 33 "We are going up to Jerusalem," he said. "The Son of Man will be handed over to the chief priests and [...] the Gentiles. 34 They will [...] kill him. Three days later he will rise from the dead!" 35 James and John [...] said, [...] 37 "Let one of us sit at your right hand in your glorious kingdom. Let the other one sit at your left hand." [...] 41 The other ten disciples [...] became angry at James and John. 42 Jesus [...] said, [...] 44 [...] "Anyone who wants to be first must be the slave of everyone. 45 Even the Son of Man did not come to be served. Instead, he came to serve others. He came to give his life as the price for setting many people free."

MIX

As they approach Jerusalem, Jesus prepares His disciples for what will happen. Jesus tells them that He will be killed and be raised from the dead in three days. However, even after hearing this, the disciples think that Jesus is going to Jerusalem to become a worldly king. As James and John ask for positions of power, Jesus tells them to serve others like He did.

MOLD

As followers of Jesus, let us not seek to be served but serve others.

BAKE

Fill in the blanks. The answers can be found in the Bible passage.

When James and John asked Jesus to let them sit at the left and right ⬤⬤⬤⬤ of His glorious kingdom, the disciples became ⬤⬤⬤⬤⬤ at them. Jesus told the disciples that whoever wants to be first must be the ⬤⬤⬤⬤⬤ of everyone, for even Jesus came to serve; not to be served.

TASTE

In this world, people think you need to be in a high position where you are served in order to be considered important. However, Jesus tells us that in God's kingdom, whoever wants to be important must be a servant of others. What kind of person do you want to be?

I want to be _____

because _____

_____

_____

PRAYER

Dear God, may my eyes not be set on positions of power but on people and places where You want me to serve and spread Your love.

31

Mark 10:46–52

I Want to See You

 PREPARE

* A rabbi is a Jewish religious leader who teaches, guides, judges, and leads worship in the Jewish community.

sticker

46 Jesus and his disciples came to Jericho. [...] A blind man was sitting by the side of the road begging. His name was Bartimaeus. [...] 47 He [...] began to shout, "Jesus! [...] Have mercy on me!" 48 Many people [...] told him to be quiet. But he shouted even louder, "Son of David! Have mercy on me!" 49 Jesus stopped and said, "Call for him." So they called out to the blind man, "Cheer up! [...] Jesus is calling for you." 50 He [...] jumped to his feet and came to Jesus. 51 "What do you want me to do for you?" Jesus asked him. The blind man said, "Rabbi, I want to be able to see." 52 "Go," said Jesus. "Your faith has healed you." Right away he could see. And he followed Jesus along the road.

MIX

While Jesus and His disciples are leaving Jericho and heading toward Jerusalem, a blind beggar named Bartimaeus hears that Jesus is passing by and calls out to Him. Although people tell him to stop, Bartimaeus calls out until Jesus hears him. Jesus calls Bartimaeus and asks what he wants. When Bartimaeus says he wants to see, Jesus heals him, and Bartimaeus follows Jesus.

MOLD

Let us call on Jesus until He opens our eyes of faith so that we could truly follow Him.

Write about your day in words and in pictures. Pray to God and express your feelings about the things He has allowed in your day and the lessons you learned from them.

BAKE

Dear God, I call to You to open my eyes of faith. Please open my eyes so that I can see You and follow You with all of my heart.

PRAYER

Time Travel with Curious Julius
A Guest at Midnight

40. The Women in the Genealogy of Jesus 5

Solomon became king over Israel, as God promised. Adonijah's evil plan to steal the throne failed, and Solomon ordered that he be killed.

Kill Adonijah!

TAN TAN

Julius couldn't solve the last question, so he ended up being stuck in between the two worlds.

Wrong!

What should I do?

NO!

Now, shall we go to meet the last woman in Jesus' genealogy?

What?

Aren't you worried about Julius?

It's not the time for time traveling!

COME ON!

To be continued...

Jesus saw their faith. So he said to the man, "Son, your sins are forgiven." (Mark 2:5)

Go through the maze to hlep the children meet Jesus.

Hide-and-Seek

Start

Finish

Choose a suitable title for today's Bible passage from the list below and share why you chose it. Write the title in the blank space at the top on the left page.

See-Saw

① Jesus forgives my sin.

② Friends help a man who cannot walk.

③ Jesus forgave the sins of a man who could not walk.

④ Faith healed a man who could not walk.

⑤ Other:

Slide

The friends of a man, who could not walk, thought and acted on their faith in Jesus. Circle the things you can do as an act of faith and put them into practice throughout the week.

Send a prayer of gratitude to God.

Do a QT devotional every day.

Give thanks before a meal.

Sing praises to God out of happiness.

CHAPTER 2

Mark 4:35–41

He got up and ordered the wind to stop. He said to the waves, "Quiet! Be still!" Then the wind died down. And it was completely calm. (Mark 4:39)

Hide-and-Seek

Find the hidden items as you meditate on today's Bible verses.

Items: cross, Bible, compass, heart, ball cap

See-Saw

Choose a suitable title for today's Bible passage from the list below and share why you chose it. Write the title in the blank space at the top on the left page.

① Jesus and His disciples encountered the storm.

② Disciples were terrified due to their lack of faith.

③ Quiet! Be still!

④ Jesus calmed the wind and the waves.

⑤ Other:

Slide

Share what scares you the most and pray the prayer below to overcome the fear.

> Dear Jesus, even the wind and the waves obey You.
>
> Please come to me and give me
>
> the strength to be brave and stay still.
>
> I pray in Your name, amen.

He told the crowd to sit down on the ground. He took the seven loaves and gave thanks to God. Then he broke them and gave them to his disciples. They passed the pieces of bread around to the people. (Mark 8:6)

Number the events in the order they happened.

Hide-and-Seek

1

See-Saw

Choose a suitable title for today's Bible passage from the list below and share why you chose it. Write the title in the blank space at the top on the left page.

① Jesus fed 4,000 people.

② Seven loaves and a few small fish

③ The people ate and were satisfied.

④ Supper with Jesus

⑤ Others:

Slide

Check the boxes below as you complete your daily devotionals and prayers.

Once more Jesus put his hands on the man's eyes. Then his eyes were opened so that he could see again. He saw everything clearly. (Mark 8:25)

Find the right words from the example to complete the Bible verses. (Mark 8:23–24)

Hide-and-Seek

[Example]

trees

eyes

people

hands

blind

V. 23 — He took the _____ man by the hand. Then he led him outside the village. He spit on the man's _____ and placed his _____ on him. "Do you see anything?" Jesus asked.

V. 24 — The man looked up. He said, "I see _____ .
They look like _____ walking around."

Choose a suitable title for today's Bible passage from the list below and share why you chose it. Write the title in the blank space at the top on the left page.

See-Saw

① A blind man in Bethsaida

② A blind man gained his sight back.

③ Jesus is the Healer.

④ Jesus placed His hands on a blind man.

⑤ Others:

 Check the boxes below as you complete your daily devotionals and prayers.

Slide

MON	TUE	WED	THU	FRI	SAT	SUN
☐	☐	☐	☐	☐	☐	☐

Answer Keys

Bible Jumble (p.15)

This is the beginning
of the good news about
Jesus the Messiah.

(Mark 1:1)

Day 02. Maze (p.21)

FOLLOWED

Day 06. Connect the Letters (p.29)

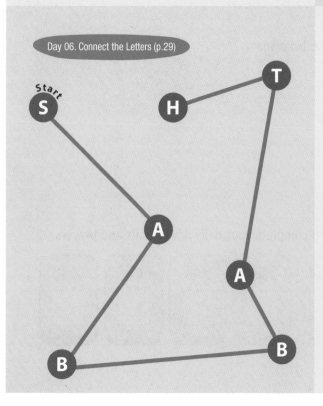

Start
S

H

T

A

A

B

B

Day 11. Connect the Boxes (p.41)

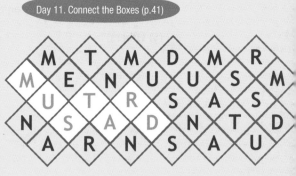

M T M D M R
M E N U U S M
U T R S A S
N S A D N T D
A R N S A U

Day 20. Word Search (p.61)

```
K F M V T R O B H X
Y I O P E N E D S Z
D E A F H T W K V U
L Y Z C R E D U E J
T O K T U E A D Q D
O N S F G D J V W H
T O N G U E E W E U
D J E B J J G M R N
J B P I R O D K O F
A O O K Q N N X S N
```

Day 27. Connect the Letters (p.77)

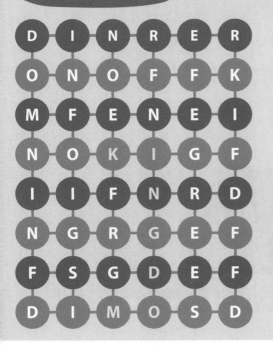

```
D  I  N  R  E  R
O  N  O  F  F  K
M  F  E  N  E  I
N  O  K  I  G  F
I  I  F  N  R  D
N  G  R  G  E  F
F  S  G  D  E  F
D  I  M  O  S  D
```

Bible Quiz (p.104)

Q. Who is the first prophet quoted in the Gospel of Mark?

3. Isaiah

Q. By what name did the demon call himself?

1. Legion

Q. What was Jesus' job?

2. Carpenter

Q. Which disciple was called from the tax collector's booth?

3. Levi

Q. How many disciples did Jesus take with Him to a high mountain?

(* Jesus took Peter, James, and John with Him.)

2. 3 disciples

THE HOLY BIBLE, NEW INTERNATIONAL READER'S VERSION®, NIRV®
Copyright © 1995, 1996, 1998, 2014 by Biblica, Inc.®
Used by Permission of Biblica, Inc.® All rights reserved worldwide.

The NIRV text may be quoted in any form (written, visual, electronic or audio), up to and inclusive of five hundred (500) verses without the express written permission of the publisher, providing the verses quoted do not amount to a complete book of the Bible nor do the verses quoted account for twenty-five percent (25%) or more of the total text of the work in which they are quoted. Permission requests that exceed the above guidelines must be directed to and approved in writing by Biblica, Inc.®, 1820 Jet Stream Drive, Colorado Springs, CO 80921, USA. Biblica.com

Notice of copyright must appear on the title or copyright page as follows:

Scripture quotations taken from The Holy Bible, New International Reader's Version ┌, NIrV®. Copyright © 1995, 1996, 1998, 2014 by Biblica, Inc.®
Used by permission of Biblica, Inc.® All rights reserved worldwide.

The "NIrV" and "New International Reader's Version" are trademarks registered in the United States Patent and Trademark Office by Biblica, Inc.®

When quotations from the NIRV text are used by a local church in non-saleable media such as church bulletins, orders of service, posters, overhead transparencies, or similar materials, a complete copyright notice is not required, but the initials (NIRV) must appear at the end of each quotation.

A portion of the purchase price of your NIRV Bible is provided to Biblica so together we support the mission of Transforming lives through God's Word.

Biblica provides God's Word to people through Bible translation & Bible publishing, and Bible engagement in Africa, Asia Pacific, Europe, Latin America, Middle East, North America, and South Asia. Through its worldwide reach, Biblica engages people with God's Word so that their lives are transformed through a relationship with Jesus Christ.

Written by **Eunhye Lee, Jihye Kim, and Elizabeth Cho**

A Red Panda Box

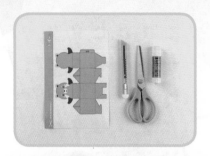

What You Need

Postcard on page 105, scissors, glue, cutter

1. Cut out the items on page 105 as shown in the picture above.

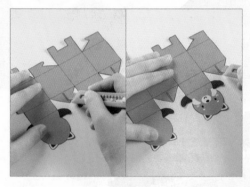

2. Cut out the white strips.

3. Fold along the dotted lines.

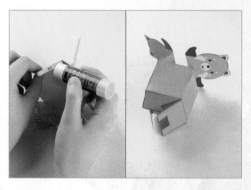

4. Apply glue to the area marked "glue" and fold it to the other side.

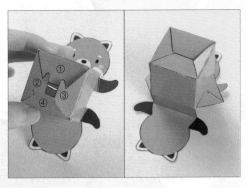

5. Fold in ①, ②, and ③ in numerical order and insert ④ underneath ① as shown in the picture above.

6. Put the arms of the panda into the slit holes.

Lesson:

Did you know red pandas are also called firefox, cat-bear, and many other names? And did you know God goes by many names like El Shaddai (Almighty) and Adonai (Lord)? As you make today's craft, thank God using all the names you know belong to Him!

When Abram was 99 years old, the LORD appeared to him. He said, "I am the Mighty God. Walk faithfully with me. Live in a way that pleases me."

(Genesis 17:1)

BIBLE QUIZ ?!

"Let's solve the Bible quiz. Ask your parents for help and solve the questions together. Have a Bible quiz time with your family. You can find the answers on page 101."

? Who is the first prophet quoted in the Gospel of Mark?

1 Jeremiah 2 Daniel
3 Isaiah

? By what name did the demon call himself?

1 Legion 2 Beelzebub
3 Baalim

? What was Jesus' job?

1 Fisherman 2 Carpenter
3 Farmer

? Which disciple was called from the tax collector's booth?

1 Mark 2 James
3 Levi

? How many disciples did Jesus take with Him to a high mountain?*

1 2 disciples 2 3 disciples
3 4 disciples